CUSTOM BIKES

MOTORCYCLE MANIA

David and Patricia Armentrout

Rourke

Publishing LLC

Vero Beach, Florida 32964

www.rourkepublishing.com

PHOTO CREDITS: Cover ©Joe Richter; title page © Greg Biggs; pp. 4, 6, 17, 21 ©Tracey Stearns; pp. 5, 22 ©Cliff Stieglitz; pp. 7 ©Thor Jorgen Udvang ; pp. 8 ©Peter Albrektsen; pp. 9 ©Jakub Semeniuk; pp. 10 ©Amy Hasenauer; pp. 12, 13 © Ford Media; pp. 15 ©Gérard Delafond; pp. 16, 18, 20 ©John L Richbourg; pp. 19 ©Michael Klenetsky; pp. 22 ©Matej Krajcovic and ©Frank Boellmann.

Title page: *Flames are a popular paint design on motorcycles.*

Editor: Robert Stengard-Olliges

Cover design by Nicola Stratford

Library of Congress Cataloging-in-Publication Data

Armentrout, David, 1962-
  Custom bikes / [David and Patricia Armentrout].
    p. cm. -- (Motorcycle mania II)
  ISBN 978-1-60044-587-3
  [1. Motorcycles--Customizing.] I. Armentrout, Patricia, 1960- II. Title.
  TL440.A7433 2008
  629.28'775--dc22

                                2007016375

Printed in the USA

CG/CG

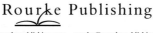

Rourke Publishing

www.rourkepublishing.com – rourke@rourkepublishing.com
Post Office Box 3328, Vero Beach, FL 32964

TABLE OF CONTENTS

ONE-OF-A-KIND MACHINES

Custom motorcycles are as unique as the people who ride them. Unlike stock motorcycles that have standard designs and are mass-produced, customs are either modified bikes or are motorcycles built to order. Custom motorcycles are one-of-a-kind.

Vivid colors and polished chrome are attention getters.

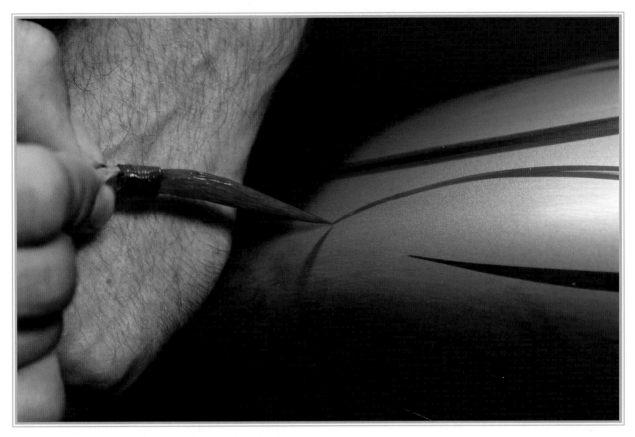

A gas tank gets a custom pinstripe.

Don't be misled by motorcycle manufacturers who use "Custom" in the model name of a mass-produced motorcycle. They are not true customs.

Most people think of choppers when it comes to custom motorcycles. A traditional chopper-style motorcycle has high handlebars, long **forks**, and a small front tire.

Choppers are all about style, rather than performance or comfort. True chopper motorcycles don't have a rear **suspension**, so they usually look a lot nicer than they ride.

A traditional looking chopper with classic black leather seat, black paint, and polished chrome.

Choppers with extended forks perform well in a straight line, but handle poorly on curves and at slow speeds.

Customizing terms like *bobber* and *chopper* were born after World War II when bikers bobbed and chopped off unnecessary parts to improve their bike's performance on the racetrack.

CUSTOMIZING VS. CUSTOMS

Customizing a motorcycle means changing something on the bike to improve its performance or to change its appearance, or both. A change can be very simple like adding a comfortable new seat, or complicated like switching out an engine or exhaust system. But bikers don't always have to change something on a motorcycle to have a custom bike. Bike builders also build custom motorcycles from the frame up.

Lots of chrome and square forks set this bike apart.

Bold colors and studded leather saddlebags customize this bike.

CUSTOM BUILDERS

The first custom bike builders were riders dissatisfied with the way their motorcycles performed or looked. Their only option was to park their bikes in the garage while they bobbed and chopped them to perfection. But now the phrase *custom bike builder* has a whole new meaning. Custom bike shops are popping up all over.

Special seats are often part of a custom bike builders design.

Custom bike builders strive for high performance and unique design.

Reality television shows like *Biker Build-Off* and *American Chopper* are a big part of the growing motorcycle culture. Besides showing how custom bikes are built, these programs are really fun to watch. Fans tune in to be entertained and to see the latest in custom motorcycle design.

The Teutul's of American Chopper fame build a custom chopper for Ford Motor Company.

Orange County Choppers is located in Montgomery, New York, and is featured on the hit TV show "American Chopper". Orange County Choppers is owned by Paul Teutul, Sr.

CLASSIC CUSTOMS

A group of European bikers created the Café Racer motorcycle in the 1950s. They modified their motorcycles to increase performance, added racing **fairings**, and adjusted the position of handlebars and footpegs. Next, they plotted a racecourse. The course began at a café, went to a predetermined point, and then back to the same café. The object was to complete the course before a song finished playing on the café's jukebox.

Modern café racers are still motorcycles that are modified for speed and handling. However, the term also describes a biker who prefers a classic British, Japanese, or Italian-made motorcycle built during the 1950s through the 1970s.

A 1950s era English racing bike.

A motorcycle frame is the backbone of the machine. The frame holds all of the bike components together, including the engine.

Frames are built from metal tubes that are bent and welded together. Sometimes the rear wheel is connected directly to the frame; sometimes to a **swing arm** that connects to the frame.

A sturdy frame supports a powerful engine.

The more cylinders in a motorcycle engine, the smoother the ride. A V-twin is a common type of two-cylinder engine. The cylinders are arranged in an angled V shape.

A two cylinder V-twin engine.

SUSPENSION

A suspension system absorbs motion caused from bumps and dips in the road. A suspension keeps a rider comfortable while helping the bike's handling. Most motorcycle suspensions include shock absorbers in the rear and telescopic forks in the front. Forks are metal tubes that connect the front wheel to the frame. Telescopic forks are a set of inner and outer tubes that slide up and down absorbing unwanted motion. **Chassis** is the suspension and frame combined.

A custom bike gets rolled out prior to a motorcycle show.

A big touring bike with heavy-duty rear shocks for comfort.

A "soft tail" motorcycle has shock absorbers in the rear that are hidden from view. A motorcycle with no rear suspension is called a hard tail. Traditional choppers have no rear suspension—OUCH!

Panels and fenders are a motorcycle's bodywork. Windshields and panels in front of the rider are called fairings. Panels that cover the engine are **cowlings**.

Not every rider wants bodywork, but for those who do it's a way to add a clean, sleek look to a motorcycle. Bikers can choose from several different molded shapes, designs, and colors—a great way to customize a ride!

A three-wheeled motorcycle is called a trike. Trikes can be built to order or customized from a kit.

A Harley-Davidson touring bike displays a biker's patriotism.

Motorcycles are technically two-wheeled vehicles, but when it comes to customizing, anything goes. A three-wheeled motorcycle is called a trike, and can be built to order or customized from a kit.

NO LIMITS

Custom builders can design and cast a set of chrome wheels or build the perfect exhaust system. Artists can complete the look by airbrushing a colorful paint design to a gas tank, or pinstripe a custom made fender.

Bikers personalize their machines with leather seats, backrests, and sissy bars. Custom-made footpegs, handgrips, and mirrors also add flair. There are really no limits to custom motorcycle design.

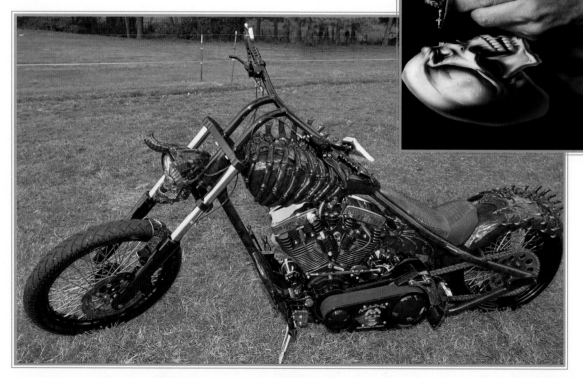

GLOSSARY

chassis (CHASS ee) — a frame and suspension system combined

cowlings (KOW lingz) — body panels that cover a motorcycle engine

fairings (FAIR ingz) — body panels that protect a motorcycle rider from the elements, such as rain and wind

forks (FORKS) — metal tubes connecting the front wheel to the rest of a motorcycle

swing arm (SWING ARM) — moveable joint that connects the rear tire, shocks, and brakes to a motorcycle frame

suspension (suh SPEN shun) — a system that absorbs shock and contributes to a motor vehicle's handling and braking

INDEX

FURTHER READING

Doeden, Matt. *Motorcycles.* Capstone Press, 2006.
Seate, Mike. *Choppers.* MBI Publishing, 2006.
Schuette, Sarah L. *Harley-Davidson Motorcycles.* Capstone Press, 2006.

WEBSITES TO VISIT

www.amadirectlink.com
www.msf-usa.org

ABOUT THE AUTHORS

David and Patricia Armentrout specialize in writing nonfiction books for young readers. They have had several books published for primary school reading. The Armentrouts live in Cincinnati, Ohio, with their two children.